STREET DANCE

THE BEST MOVES

DJ HOOCH

STREET DANCE

THE BEST MOVES

DJ HOOCH

CASSELL ILLUSTRATED

CONTENTS

WHAT IS STREET DANCE?

WHERE IT STARTED

Street dance is the broad term that's used to describe a number of different types of dance that originated outside of a dance studio – usually on the streets, but also in clubs, parks, and other open spaces…

While it's tricky to trace the very first type of street dance, because forms of it exist the world over, the precursor to what we now know as street dance is African-American dance. This style of dance developed within communities who were brought to the United States as slaves during the early 19th century.

Early styles of street dance include:

▶ Folk
▶ Tap
▶ Traditional jazz

What we now see on TV and in films referred to as 'street dance' is a mixture of moves from different forms of styles: bboy, popping, locking, hip hop, and house. These styles emerged back in the 1960s and '70s across the USA.

It was a time when gang warfare was rife. In the middle of these troubled times, a DJ from the South Bronx, Afrika Bambaataa, recognized that there was a need for a way to channel energy towards something positive and creative, towards activities that engaged young people but also gave them an opportunity to express themselves.

BBOYING (OR BREAKING)

Bambaataa saw the potential for this in what we now know as the culture of hip hop. Hip hop traditionally has four elements: bboying, DJing, graffiti, and MCing. These different elements, which require physical, mental, and creative energy, became ways for rivalries to be played out without resorting to violence.

From Bambaataa's founding principles, hip hop became a global cultural movement. DJ Kool Herc named the dancers bboys because they danced on the break of the beat, and Bambaataa founded one of the first-known bboy crews that he called the Zulu Kings.

LOCKING

Locking was a dance invented by street dancer Don Campbell in the late 1960s, and pioneered by his dance group The Lockers, famous for appearing as the house dancers on legendary TV show *Soul Train.*

As a style locking is visually distinctive, with traditional outfits including baggy pants, newsboy/barrowboy caps, and stripes in abundance. Musically, they dance to funky soul and disco.

POPPING

The dance style of popping originated on the West Coast of America in the 1970s, thanks to a dancer called Boogaloo Sam, who was inspired to develop his own styles of dance after seeing The Lockers on TV. These styles became known as popping and boogaloo. Popping got its name from the way the dancer contracts or 'hits' his or her muscles to the beat of the music to create a snapping, or jerking, effect.

Poppers originally danced to a mix of funk and disco, particularly acts like Parliament, Zapp, and Cameo. By the early 1980s they were also using the electro tracks being produced by acts such as Soul Sonic Force, Kraftwerk, Jonzun Crew, and The Extra T's.

HOUSE

One of the more recent forms of street dance, house dance originated in the post-disco era in clubs in both New York and Chicago. The dance style is heavily social, with the emphasis on freestyling and vibing to the music played by the DJ.

The music that house style is danced to now includes soulful house, broken beats, and minimal tech.

HIP HOP

As the breaking craze died out in New York and the style of rap music changed, a new dance style arose in the clubs: hip hop freestyle. Like other forms of street dance, this was heavily influenced by the music coming out at the time. The Cabbage Patch, for example, is linked to the song of the same name by Gucci Crew II, which described the moves.

STREET DANCE TODAY

While each style has remained individual, they all have the same social spirit and competitive drive behind them, now often being seen together at parties and jams, as well as staged at big competitions across the world. Although these styles mostly started out in America, they are now practised pretty much everywhere you go in the world.

TV and the internet have helped spread awareness of these dance styles, and made superstars of some of the leading dancers. You can check out dancers like France's Lilou and Korea's Hong10 (breaking), Les Twins and Salah from France and Paradox from Holland (hip hop), Greenteck from Canana and Go Go Brothers from Japan (locking), and Yugson and Kapella from France (house) on YouTube if you want to see some of the best in the world doing their stuff.

Throughout the book, as well as the step-by-step photos and instructions, you will be able to use your smartphone or tablet to access videos of each move so you can make sure you're doing it properly.

Street dances are for everyone, so give them all a go, see which one you like and get stuck in.

DJ Hooch

Founder of the UK Bboy Championships

BBOY

WHAT IS IT?

Through this section, we'll show you how to do key signature moves including: Toprock (upright moves), Footwork (moves when you're on the ground), and Freezes (held positions). Within each of these moves there are different variations that you can try out and combine. On page 40 you can check out what tracks to dance to once you're feeling confident.

To help you and to keep you motivated while you learn, we have tips from our breaking experts Roxy and Sunni throughout.

THE MOVES

INDIAN STEP

THIS IS A BASIC TOPROCK MOVE, AND THE MOST COMMONLY USED, SO IT'S A GOOD ONE TO GET YOU STARTED.

01

02

03

Start with your feet shoulder-width apart and your arms crossed in front of your body at waist height.

Step your right leg forwards diagonally across your body, and open your arms in a diagonal with the left arm raised, right arm lowered.

Step your right foot back into the starting position and cross your arms.

04

Step your left leg forwards diagonally across your body, and open your arms in a diagonal with the right arm raised and left arm lowered.

05

Return to the starting position, with your arms resting by your sides.

3-STEP

STEPS 2, 3, AND 4 ARE THE 3 STEPS THAT GAVE THIS MOVE ITS NAME. WE'VE INCLUDED THE START AND FINISH POSITIONS, PLUS A REPETITION TO SHOW HOW YOU CIRCLE ROUND.

01

Start with your knees bent and your weight resting on your raised heels.

02

Extend your left leg out in front of you and place your left hand on the floor.

03

Swing your left leg in a circular motion behind you. Place both hands on the floor in front of you as you do so, and jump your legs out.

04

05

Lean to the left slightly and, with a gentle hop, switch arms so your left hand is placed on the ground and your right comes across your body. Your legs also switch so your right leg tucks in beneath you and your left leg shoots out.

Bring your left leg back in and bend it so you are resting on your left heel. At the same time, shoot your right leg out between your left leg and right arm, and then lift your left arm across your body.

06

07

08

Repeat step 3.

Repeat step 4.

Bring your right leg back in so you are crouching again and rest your arms on your knees.

6-STEP

SUNNI SAYS, 'MAKE SURE THIS IS A CONTINUOUS, CIRCULAR, SYMMETRICAL MOVEMENT, ONCE YOU'VE PRACTISED IT A FEW TIMES.' WE'VE INCLUDED THE START POSITION FOR YOU.

Start with your knees bent and your weight resting on your raised heels.

Place your right hand on the floor, roughly in line with your feet, to help you balance. Note, your palm should not be flat on the floor: your fingers should be pressed together, flat on the floor, with your thumb separated out as a support. Your free arm can be in varying positions, whatever feels natural – resting on your hip or crossing your body with your hand on your right shoulder, for example.

03 Move your right leg across and in front of your bent left leg. The sole of your right foot should be facing out. This is the first part of the 6-Step. Step your left leg backwards until both of your legs are almost straight, but not locked.

04 Place your left hand on the floor and move your right leg back so that it is mirroring the left leg. Your knees should be slightly bent, and you should be on your toes.

05 Lift your right arm up to your hip and step your left leg forwards and across your right leg. This should be the mirror of step 3 (the second part of the 6-Step).

06 Bring your right foot forwards, bending the leg so the foot tucks in behind your left knee.

07 Bring your left leg round in front of you so you are once again in the starting position.

TOE-HEEL CROSS

SUNNI SAYS, 'MAKE SURE YOU USE YOUR ARMS TO EMPHASIZE THE MOVEMENT. IT'S PART OF YOUR TOPROCK MOVES SO IT SHOULD BE AS FUNKY AS POSSIBLE.'

01

Start with your feet hip-width apart and arms resting at your sides.

02

Twist your body slightly to the left, with a slight bend in the left knee and touch the toe of your right foot to the floor. Keep your arms loose so they can follow the movement of your body.

03

Rotate your hips to the right and, as your feet move to point towards the right, your right foot rocks from front to back, so the heel is now on the floor, rather than the toe.

04

Still facing forwards, step across your body with your right leg, so your weight is now on your right foot.

05

Give a small hop on your right leg, bringing your left leg out to the left-hand side of your body, and mirror step 2, touching your left toe to the floor.

06

Turn your hips to the left and, as your feet move to point to the left, your left foot rocks from front to back, so the heel is now on the floor rather than the toe.

07

Still facing forwards, step across your body with your left leg, so your weight is now on your left foot.

08

Hop on your left leg, bringing your right leg out to the right-hand side of your body, with your arms resting on your hips.

09

Step your feet and arms back to the centre.

DOUBLE BREATHER

THIS TOPROCK MOVE IS UPRIGHT AND JERKY, BUT IT ALLOWS YOU TO USE THE BEAT OF THE MUSIC TO GOOD EFFECT. WATCH THE VIDEO TO CHECK YOU'RE DOING IT RIGHT!

01

Start with your feet shoulder-width apart and your arms resting by your sides.

02

Kick your right leg forwards and cross your arms.

03

Jump your weight on to your right leg, and kick the left leg forwards.

04

Jump forwards on to your left leg, opening your arms, and tuck your right foot behind your left leg.

05

Step backwards with your right leg so your weight is on your right foot, leaving the left leg straight in front of you. Cross your arms.

06

Jump and change your legs so your weight is now on your left leg.

07

Jump forwards on to your right leg, opening your arms, and tuck your left foot behind your right leg.

08

Step back on to your left leg, from where you can repeat the move from step 2.

WATCH THE › ‹ VIDEO HERE

SALSA STEP

TOPROCK INCORPORATES LOTS OF DIFFERENT STYLES, INCLUDING SALSA. THIS MOVE IS ALSO KNOWN AS THE LATIN ROCK.

01

Start with your feet shoulder-width apart and arms resting by your sides.

02

Kick your right leg out in front of you, at the same time punching your arms forwards with your hands in loose fists. Alternatively, you can just punch one arm forwards (alternating between the left and right).

03

Bring your arms into your body at chest height, bending at the elbow, and lower your right leg as you prepare to change legs.

04

Step your left leg out to the left and lower your foot to the ground, while opening your arms to the right. Your left arm should be in front of you and your right arm out at a right angle to it.

05

Step your left leg back to the centre and then, in a mirror of step 2, kick your left leg out in front of you while punching your arms forwards with your hands in loose fists.

06

Bring your arms in to your body at chest height, bending at the elbow, and lower your left leg as you prepare to change legs.

07

Step your right leg out to the right and lower your foot to the ground, while opening your arms to the left. Your right arm should be in front of you and your left arm out at a right angle to it.

08

Step your right leg back to the centre and lower your arms to rest by your sides.

INDIAN STEP VARIATION

THERE ARE LOTS OF DIFFERENT VARIATIONS YOU CAN DO ON YOUR TOPROCK MOVES. HERE'S ONE FOR THE INDIAN STEP.

01

Start with your feet shoulder-width apart and arms resting by your sides.

02

Kick your right leg out in front of you, at the same time punching your arms forwards with your hands in loose fists. Alternatively, you can just punch one arm forwards (alternating between the left and right).

03

Bring your arms into your body at chest height, bending at the elbow, and lower your right leg as you prepare to change legs.

04

Step your left leg forwards across your right leg and raise your right arm up to your head in a salute. Push your left arm behind you for balance.

05

Step your left leg back to the centre and then, in a mirror of step 2, kick your left leg out in front of you while punching your arms forwards with your hands in loose fists.

06

Bring your arms in to your body at chest height, bending at the elbow, and lower your left leg as you prepare to change legs.

07

Step your right leg forwards across your left leg and raise your left arm up to your head in a salute. Push your right arm behind you for balance.

08

Step your right leg back to the centre and lower your arms to rest by your sides.

WATCH THE › [QR code] ‹ VIDEO HERE

CCs

ROXY SAYS, 'CCS IS A GOOD FOUNDATION FOOTWORK MOVE TO KNOW.' IF YOU'RE WONDERING, CCS STANDS FOR CRAZY COMMANDOS, AFTER THE CREW WHO MADE THEM POPULAR.

01

Start with your knees bent, and your weight resting on your raised heels. Placing your right hand on the floor beside you, and keeping your arm straight, lean on your right arm and stretch your right leg out in front of you, turning your body to the right as you do so.

02

When you have turned your body enough to do so, put both hands on the floor. Keeping your right foot in contact with the floor, kick out with your left heel.

03

Rotate your body left so you are back in the same position as you were in step 1.

04

Now reverse the move. Put your left hand on the floor, keeping your arm straight. With a slight hop, switch legs so your right leg is bent beneath you and your left leg is straight out in front of you.

05

Turning your body to the left, place both hands on the floor and kick out with your right heel.

06

Rotate your body right so you are back in the same position as you were in step 4.

WATCH THE › ‹ VIDEO HERE

BACK SPIN

THIS IS A MORE ADVANCED MOVE, SO MAKE SURE YOU ARE NICELY WARMED UP. SUNNI SAYS, 'START SLOWLY AT FIRST AND, IF YOU GET THE HANG OF IT, BUILD UP MOMENTUM.'

01

Start sitting on the floor, with your right hand placed on the floor behind you, and your legs open in a split towards the right.

02

Lean backwards as you swing your left leg in a circular motion all the way until you are on your back.

03

Keeping your legs together, lift them up from the waist and towards your body. Try to stay quite high on your back.

04

Cross your feet at the ankles as you bring your knees in to your body and wrap your arms behind your knees in a hugging motion.

05

Use your momentum to keep spinning round...

06

... Keep spinning.

WATCH THE › ‹ VIDEO HERE

BABY FREEZE

THIS FIRST VERSION IS A SIMPLIFIED BABY FREEZE IN WHICH YOU KEEP ONE FOOT ON THE FLOOR TO HELP YOU BALANCE.

01

Start by kneeling down and placing your head sideways on the ground to the right of your body, making sure your face doesn't touch the floor. Press your right elbow squarely into your hip. Reach your left arm in front of you and place your hand on the floor in front of you, elbow bent, fingers splayed and palm raised. When you feel comfortable, lift your left leg up and bend it back at the knee. Keep your right foot on the floor at all times.

02

When you are comfortable in this position, you can lift your left hand and place it on your waist.

THIS SECOND VERSION IS A REGULAR BABY FREEZE. MAKE SURE YOU FEEL AT EASE DOING THE SIMPLIFIED VERSION BEFORE ATTEMPTING THIS.

01

Repeat step 1 of the Baby Freeze. From this position, bring your right leg in and rest your knee on your left elbow.

02

From step 1, you can change the position of your legs to make variations of the Baby Freeze, like tucking your left leg behind your right knee as shown here.

WATCH THE › ‹ VIDEO HERE

CHAIR FREEZE

FREEZES ARE A COOL WAY TO FINISH OFF MOVES. ROXY SAYS, 'MAKE SURE YOU DON'T PUT YOUR FACE TO THE FLOOR OR YOU MIGHT HURT YOUR NECK!'

01

Start by kneeling down and placing your head sideways on the ground to the right of your body, making sure your face doesn't touch the floor. Press your right elbow squarely into your hip, straighten your left leg out, bend it at the knee and place your foot on the floor. Once you feel comfortable, raise your right leg up and rest your right foot on your left knee. Finally, lift your left arm and place your hand at your waist.

02

You can change positions to create variations of the Chair Freeze. For example, change legs to create the reverse Chair Freeze.

03

You can take your left hand off your waist and extend your left arm back behind your head so your hand can reach out to the floor.

!

This is how NOT to position yourself for a Freeze. Be careful and make sure you are comfortable in the starting position before attempting to vary it.

RUSSIANS

THIS IS A NICE BBOY MOVE, WHICH LOOKS A BIT LIKE RUSSIAN COSSACK DANCING, HENCE THE NAME.

01

Start in a crouching position with your arms resting on your thighs.

02

With your right arm behind you, place your fingers firmly on the floor with the palm raised. Your left arm will come across your body as though reaching to your right shoulder. At the same time, jump your legs forwards, with your right leg straight out to the front, and your left leg out at a 45-degree angle to the left.

03

Jump back to the centre.

04

With your left arm behind you, place your fingers firmly on the floor with the palm raised. Your right arm will come across your body as though reaching to your left shoulder. At the same time, jump your legs forwards, with your left leg straight out in front, and your right leg out at a 45-degree angle to the right.

05

Jump back to the centre.

DJ HOOCH'S TOP 10 TRACKS

For each style of street dance in the book there are 10 tracks to get you started. They represent just a fraction of the music out there to dance to, so once you've got into these gems, start diggin' for more tunes in all the genres you like. Remember, the music is your guide. Listen not just to the beats, but to the rhythms and melodies to really master your moves!

INCREDIBLE BONGO BAND – 'APACHE'

BABE RUTH – 'THE MEXICAN'

JAMES BROWN - 'GIVE IT UP TURN IT LOOSE'

JIMMY CASTOR – 'JUST BEGUN'

CAVERN – 'LIQUID LIQUID'

MANU DIBANGO – 'AFRICAN BATTLE'

THE MOHAWKS – 'THE CHAMP'

ISAAC HAYES – 'DISCO CONNECTION'

RUFUS THOMAS – 'ITCH AND SCRATCH'

BADDER THAN EVIL – 'HOT WHEELS'

WHAT'S GOOD TO WEAR?

FOOTWEAR
LET'S START WITH THE FEET! BBOYS AND BGIRLS TEND TO WEAR CLASSIC SNEAKERS:
PUMA SUEDES, ADIDAS SUPERSTARS, CONVERSE ALL STARS, NIKE HUARACHES...
IF YOU DON'T HAVE ANY OF THESE, JUST MAKE SURE YOU WEAR COMFORTABLE
SNEAKERS OR SPORTS SHOES THAT WILL SUPPORT YOU.

CLOTHING
YOU'VE GOT TO BE FREE TO MOVE AROUND EASILY, SO TRACKSUIT BOTTOMS,
LOOSE-FITTING JEANS (OR JEANS WITH STRETCH), OR LONG, LOOSE SHORTS.
KEEP IT SIMPLE UP TOP WITH A T-SHIRT, SWEATSHIRT, OR TRACKSUIT TOP.

HEADWEAR
IF YOU WANT TO GO OLD SCHOOL, WEAR A KANGOL CAP, BUT ANY CAP OR A
HEADSPIN BEANIE WILL DO.

POPPING

WHAT IS IT?

As we said in the introduction to this book, popping originated on West Coast America in the 1970s. To create the popping effect, the dancers contract their muscles, which results in the robotic style of movement. In this chapter, we're going to take a look at how to master this funk dance of robotic isolation, mime, and musicality.

We've got renowned dancer Brooke Milliner showing you the moves here, and he also offers some tips along the way. Check out page 62 for my essential tracks to dance to.

THE MOVES

WATCH THE › [QR code] ‹ VIDEO HERE

WALK OUT

THIS IS A BASIC MOVE OF POPPING, WHICH HELPS YOU GET FROM POINT A TO B.

01

Stand with arms resting down and your feet aligned beneath your hips.

02

Keeping your legs straight, lean your torso slightly to the right, raising your right shoulder a couple of inches at the same time.

03

Keeping your right leg straight, step forwards diagonally with your right foot, bending the stationary left leg slightly at the knee. At the same time as this forwards diagonal move, raise your left arm, keeping it bent at the elbow so your arm is in a right angle. Your right arm moves backwards slightly to compensate.

04

Step your left foot forwards so your feet are aligned and your arms are resting by your sides.

WATCH THE › ‹ VIDEO HERE

DOUBLE WALK OUT

THE DOUBLE WALK OUT IS AN EXTENDED VERSION OF THE WALK OUT (ON PAGES 44–45).

01

Stand with arms resting down and your feet aligned beneath your hips.

02

Keeping your legs straight, lean your torso slightly to the right, raising your right shoulder a couple of inches at the same time.

03

Step forwards diagonally with your right foot. At the same time, raise your left arm, keeping it bent so your arm is in a right angle. Your right arm moves backwards slightly.

Keeping your right leg straight, bring it in a circular motion round to the right of your body, leading with your heel slightly raised off the ground. When your leg reaches a 45-degree angle, lower your foot to the floor. At the same time as your leg is doing this circular motion, bring your right arm, bent at the elbow, across your body to your left-hand side, so it is parallel with your left arm.

Your body should have reached a stop in this position.

Turn your torso and head in a fixed position to the right, until they are parallel with your right leg.

Pivot on the ball of your left foot towards the right, raising the left heel.

Step your left leg forwards, bringing it in line with your right leg, and drop your arms to finish the move.

WATCH THE › ‹ VIDEO HERE

EGYPTIAN TWIST

WHEN YOU'VE PRACTISED THIS MOVE A FEW TIMES, YOU'LL SEE WHY IT'S CALLED THE EGYPTIAN TWIST – THE MOVES ECHO ANCIENT EGYPTIAN DANCERS.

01

Stand with your feet together and arms resting by your sides.

02

With your fingers stretched out towards the floor, lift your heels and turn them to the right until they reach a 45-degree angle, taking care not to twist your body at the same time.

03

Keeping the movement continuous, lower the heels to the floor, raise your left shoulder slightly and the palms of your hands until they are parallel with the floor and your fingers are pointing outwards.

04

Pivot on your heels so that your toes point to the right, while raising your right shoulder slightly and dropping your left shoulder.

05

Bring your right shoulder back down and bend your knees slightly while raising your heels off the floor.

06

Pivot left on your toes and lower your heels to the floor with a slight raise of the left shoulder.

07

Bring your heels back to the centre so your feet are facing forwards, drop your left shoulder and lower your hands to your sides to finish the move.

WATCH THE › ‹ VIDEO HERE

FRESNO

THIS MOVE WAS INVENTED BY A DANCER CALLED BOOGALOO SAM. BROOKE SAYS, 'USE THIS MOVE TO HELP YOU LEARN HOW TO POP YOUR MUSCLES TO THE BEAT.'

01

Stand straight with your feet hip-width apart and arms resting by your sides.

02

Keeping your right arm straight, bring it upwards, while at the same time turning your left heel towards the right foot.

03

As your arm is still lifting, pivot slightly on the ball of the right foot so your feet are parallel. Your arm should hit shoulder height as your legs reach parallel position. Pop the arm as it reaches this point.

04

Lower your right arm and turn your right heel inward, while simultaneously raising your left arm.

05

As your left arm is lifting, pivot slightly to the right on the ball of your left foot so your feet are parallel. Your left arm should reach shoulder height as your legs reach parallel position. Pop the arm as it reaches this point.

06

Lower your left arm and turn your left heel inward to finish the move.

WATCH THE › ‹ VIDEO HERE

MASTER FLEX

EACH POSITION IN THE MASTER FLEX MOVE IS A STOP, SO MAKE SURE YOU HIT EACH STEP CLEANLY.

01 Stand straight with your feet together and your arms by your sides.

02 Keeping both legs straight, raise your right leg while bringing your left arm up, bent at the elbow, to a right angle. Keep your fingers straight. Your right arm will move back slightly.

03 Swing your right leg back and put your toe on the ground. At the same time, bring your arms in to your sides and lean your torso backwards, so it is in line with your left leg.

04

Move your torso forwards, leading from the head, and swing your arms forwards until they are at a 180-degree angle to the floor.

05

Bend both knees slightly, while raising your arms from the elbows until they form right angles.

06

Keeping your arms out to the sides, twist your torso 90 degrees to the right, keeping your head and feet facing forwards.

07

Turn your head to the right, while pivoting on the balls of your feet.

08

Stop when you are facing the opposite direction to step 1. Your arms should still be at right angles to your body, your left heel raised and your right foot flat on the floor.

09

Step your left foot forwards, bringing it in line with your right foot, and lower your arms to your sides to finish the move.

WATCH THE › [QR code] ‹ VIDEO HERE

NECK O'FLEX

IF YOU GET THIS MOVE RIGHT, IT'LL LOOK LIKE YOUR HEAD AND BODY ARE MOVING INDEPENDENTLY OF EACH OTHER!

01

Start with your feet together and hands by your sides.

02

Rotate your head, bringing it slightly forwards and turning it to the left until it is in line with your left shoulder.

03

Turn your torso towards the left so it is in line with your head. As you are turning, step first your left foot, then your right foot. Keep your head still.

04

Continue turning, rotating 180 degrees. Your feet should be together and arms by your sides, but your head still turned in the same direction, now in line with your right shoulder.

05

Rotate your head, bringing it slightly forwards and turning it to the left so it is in line with your left shoulder.

06

Turn your torso towards the left so it is in line with your head. As you are turning, step first your left foot, then your right foot. Again, keep your head still.

07

Continue turning, rotating 180 degrees. Your body should be facing forwards, feet together and arms by your sides, but your head still turned in the same direction, now in line with your right shoulder.

08

Rotate your head left to the centre.

WATCH THE › ‹ VIDEO HERE

OLD MAN

BOOGALOO SAM CAME UP WITH THIS MOVE AFTER WATCHING AN ELDERLY MAN WALKING ACROSS THE STREET. HE EXAGGERATED THE MOVEMENT TO CREATE THIS FUNKY STEP.

01 Start with your feet together and your hands resting by your sides.

02 In a circular motion, bring your right leg backwards until it reaches a 45-degree angle. At the same time, your left shoulder should raise slightly.

03 Bring your right leg forwards, lower your left shoulder and raise your right shoulder slightly.

04

Continue to move your right leg forwards until it reaches a 45-degree angle. Keeping your leg straight with the foot flexed and heel raised, move the foot out to the right in a circular motion.

05

As your right foot is placed back down, bend your left leg slightly and raise your left shoulder.

06

Shift your weight to the right by bending your right leg and straightening out your left leg. As you do this, raise your right shoulder.

07

Step your left foot in so it is next to your right foot and both knees are slightly bent.

08

Step your right leg out towards the right, and bend your left leg, slightly raising your left shoulder.

09

Step your right foot back in so it is parallel with your left foot, and straighten up. Let your hands rest by your sides.

WATCH THE › ‹ VIDEO HERE

ROMEO TWIST

THIS MOVE CREATES A ROBOTIC ILLUSION WITH HANDS AND FEET MOVING TOGETHER TO EXAGGERATE THE DIRECTION AND FLOW. MOVE WITH THE BEAT OF THE MUSIC.

01

Stand straight with your hands resting down by your sides.

02

Bend forwards at the waist until you reach a 90-degree angle, keeping your arms loose and dropping towards the floor, with your hands straight.

03

Move both hands at the wrist simultaneously to the left.

04

Stop when your hands reach a 90-degree angle, but as they are moving, turn the toe of your right foot in 45 degrees so it is pointing at your left foot.

05

Reverse the hand movement in steps 3 and 4, so they are rotated 180 degrees towards the right, and turn the toe of your right foot out to the right until it reaches a 45-degree angle.

06

Rotate your hands back towards the left again, lifting the heel of your right foot as you do so and pivoting on the ball of the foot.

07

Stop when your hands reach a 90-degree angle towards the left and your right foot, once again, points in towards the left foot.

08

Bring your left foot in so it is next to your right and both feet are facing forwards. Straighten up your torso and let your hands rest by your sides.

WATCH THE › ‹ VIDEO HERE

TW1ST O'FLEX

BROOKE SAYS, 'FOR THIS MOVE YOU NEED TO THINK OF EACH BIT OF YOUR BODY MOVING INDEPENDENTLY OF THE OTHERS. TAKE IT SLOW TO START WITH.'

01

Stand up straight with your feet together and your hands resting by your sides.

02

Bending your arms at the elbows, raise them until they are at right angles to your body. Your thumbs should be separated out from your fingers.

03

Step your right foot backwards as your arms begin to lower.

04

Step back with your left foot so it is in line with your right foot, and as the arms lower, rest your hands on your waist.

05

Keeping your arms in this position, rotate your shoulders and hands left, so your right hand is at your stomach and your left hand is at the small of your back.

06

Raise the heel of your right foot, keeping the ball of the foot on the ground, and bending the right knee slightly.

07

Turn your head and torso to the left, and pivot on the ball of your right foot towards the left until you have turned 90 degrees.

08

Step your right foot forwards to meet your left and lower your hands to rest at your sides.

DJ HOOCH'S TOP 10 TRACKS

PARLIAMENT – 'FLASHLIGHT'

CARL CARLTON – 'SHE'S BAD MAMA JAMA'

RAY PARKER JR – 'STILL IN THE GROOVE'

YOUNG AND COMPANY – 'I LIKE (WHAT YOU ARE DOING TO ME)'

LENNY WHITE & TWENNYNINE – 'PEANUT BUTTER'

T-CONNECTION – 'ANYTHING GOES'

ONE WAY – 'GET UP'

LAKESIDE – 'IT'S ALL THE WAY LIVE'

FATBACK – 'BACKSTROKIN''

DAZZ BAND – 'KEEP IT LIVE'

WHAT'S GOOD TO WEAR?

FOOTWEAR
AS WITH BBOY DANCEWEAR, YOU CAN WEAR SNEAKERS (USUALLY AIR FORCE ONE NIKE OR ADIDAS GAZELLES), OR HUSH PUPPIES IF YOU HAVE THEM.

CLOTHING
ANYTHING THAT ALLOWS YOU FREEDOM OF MOVEMENT BUT STILL CLEARLY SHOWS THE MOVES YOU'RE DOING. CLOTHESWISE THIS IS A MORE RELAXED STYLE THAN BBOY, SO USUALLY LOOSE, BAGGY JEANS OR TROUSERS. TRADITIONALLY, DANCERS WOULD WEAR A LOOSE-FITTING DRESS SHIRT OR JACKET. NOW THEY'RE MORE LIKELY TO WEAR A LOOSE-FITTING T-SHIRT, OFTEN LONG-SLEEVED.

HEADWEAR
NO SPINNING GOING ON HERE, SO ANYTHING FROM TRILBY HATS TO BOWLERS AND CAPS.

LOCKING

WHAT IS IT?

Put your funky shoes on and try out the moves on the next few pages. Pretty soon you'll know your Skeeter Rabbit from your Scoo B Doo. For references on music to lock to, check out page 80, and read about some of the amazing outfits lockers wear on page 81.

THE MOVES

CARTOON HEAD TURN

THIS MOVE IS ALL ABOUT ISOLATING THE NECK, SO MAKE SURE YOU'RE NICE AND LOOSE BEFORE YOU START.

01

Stand straight with your head facing forwards.

02

Extend your neck forwards and smoothly turn your head to the left, moving from the neck, until you reach a 90-degree angle.

03

Retract your neck back in and stop.

Extend your neck forwards again.

With your neck still extended, smoothly turn your head to the left, moving from the neck, until you reach a 90-degree angle.

Retract your neck and stand straight.

WATCH THE › ‹ **VIDEO HERE**

POINTS

IT'S PRETTY OBVIOUS WHY THESE ARE CALLED POINTS!
BROOKE SAYS, 'KEEP EVERY STEP NICE AND CLEAN, AND
CLEARLY SEPARATED.'

01 Stand straight with your arms resting by your sides.

02 Lift your right arm across your body, bending at the elbow, with your fist clenched and your first finger pointed to the right.

03 Extend your right arm out from the elbow until it is pointing straight out to the right.

Bring your right arm in, bending at the elbow, and retracting your first finger into the fist. When your arm is halfway in to your body, rotate your elbow down and bring it in to your side. As you straighten your right arm down towards the floor, lift your left arm across your body, bending at the elbow, with your fist clenched and your first finger pointed.

Your right arm should now be straight down by your side and your left arm pointing right across your body, elbow at shoulder height, your first finger pointed.

Extend your left arm out from the elbow until it is pointing straight out to the left.

Bring your left arm in, bending at the elbow, and retracting your first finger into the fist. When your arm is halfway in to your body, rotate your elbow down and bring it in to your side.

Drop both arms to rest by your sides. You should now be back in the starting position.

SCOOBOT

A DANCER CALLED JIMMY 'SCOO B DOO' FOSTER CREATED THIS FUNKY STEP. IT INVOLVES A LOT OF MOVEMENT IN A SMALL SPACE, SO GET READY TO WORK THOSE MUSCLES...

01

Stand straight with your arms resting by your sides.

02

Lift your right arm at the elbow until it reaches shoulder height.

Lean to the right as you extend your right arm and kick your left leg out to the side.

Lower your left leg so you are upright with both arms bent at the elbow.

Cross your arms while lifting your right leg up and out. At the same time, move your right shoulder forwards and to the left.

As you continue to lift your right leg up and out to the right in a kick, extend your crossed arms down in front of you.

Rotate your body back round to the centre. Lower your right leg and uncross your arms, but keep them bent at the elbows with fists clenched.

Raise your arms — still keeping them bent at the elbows - until they are at right angles to your body. At the same time, straighten your back, bringing your right leg in and foot down. Stop in this position.

Fold your arms in at the elbows, bringing your fists down and elbows up.

10

Raising your fists and extending your arms up and out, start a circular motion, gradually unclenching your fists. Continue the circular movement down.

11

Bring your arms down and behind your back. As your arms move behind your back, bring your hands together in a clap to finish the move.

WATCH THE › ‹ **VIDEO HERE**

SCOO B DOO

THIS IS ANOTHER MOVE THOUGHT UP BY JIMMY 'SCOO B DOO' FOSTER.

01

Stand straight with your arms resting by your sides and your feet together.

02

Raise your arms with your elbows bent until they're at right angles to your body.

03

Return your arms to your sides.

04

Bring your elbows out and up until they are at right angles to your body. As you are doing this, round your back, bringing the shoulders slightly forwards. At the same time, turn the toes of your feet out at 45 degrees, keeping the heels together, and bend your knees outwards.

05

Straighten your right leg, and raise your left knee. At the same time, straighten and lower your left arm and bring your right elbow into your body, raising your right fist to chest height.

06

Lower your right arm in front of you. Flick the wrist with a bounce in the arm. Bring your left leg forwards in a kick to coincide with the wrist flick.

07

Hop so that your weight is on your left leg and raise your right knee. Your arms should now be down by your sides.

08

Simultaneously lower your right leg to the floor and start to raise your left arm at the elbow. Stop your arm when you reach this position.

SKEETER RABBIT

AS THE NAME MIGHT SUGGEST, THERE'S LOTS OF JUMPING AROUND IN THIS MOVE. IT WAS INVENTED BY JAMES 'SKEETER RABBIT' HIGGINS.

01 Stand straight with your arms resting by your sides.

02 Raise your right arm at the elbow while kicking your left leg out to the front. From here, jump both feet forwards and 45 degrees to the right into step 3.

03 Land your jump with elbows tucked in to your body. Keep your fists clenched.

04

Jump your feet apart while at the same time raising your left arm at the elbow.

05

Jump back to the centre, facing forwards again, with your weight on your right leg, keeping your left leg lifted and bent at the knee. At the same time, your right arm raises at the elbow and your left arm lowers.

06

Lower your right arm at the elbow, straight in front of you, flicking the wrist with a bounce in the arm before lowering it to your side. At the same time, bring your left leg forwards in a kick, which should coincide with the wrist flick.

07

Hop so that your weight is on your left leg and raise your right knee. Then, simultaneously lower your right foot to the floor and start to raise your left arm at the elbow.

08

Stop your arm when you reach this position.

WATCH THE › [QR code] ‹ VIDEO HERE

GIVE YA'SELF 5

THIS MOVE IS ALL IN THE ARMS AND HANDS. LIKE THE NAME SAYS, YOU'RE BASICALLY GIVING YOURSELF 5.

01

Start with your arms resting by your sides.

02

Keeping your elbow tucked in by your side, rotate your right arm round and out to the right. Your hand should remain flat with your palm facing upwards.

03

Rotate your bent right arm left to cross your body.

04

Raise your left arm at the elbow while slightly lowering the right arm, straightening out your wrist and fingers.

05

Bring your hands together in a clap.

06

Follow the clap through, so your left arm falls down by your side.

07

Lower your right arm to your side.

DJ HOOCH'S TOP 10 TRACKS

B.T. EXPRESS – 'ENERGY LEVEL'

BOHANNON – 'LET'S START THE DANCE'

JAMES BROWN – 'RAPP PAYBACK'

SLY & THE FAMILY STONE – 'DANCE TO THE MUSIC'

THE SOUL SEARCHERS – 'BLOW YOUR WHISTLE'

SUN – 'SUN IS HERE'

VERNON BUNCH – 'GET UP'

ISAAC HAYES – 'DISCO CONNECTION'

KOOL & THE GANG – 'RATED X'

DENNIS COFFEY – 'SCORPIO'

WHAT'S GOOD TO WEAR?

FOOTWEAR
TRADITIONALLY LOCKING DANCERS WORE TWO-TONE SHOES.
BUT NOW SNEAKERS ARE JUST AS COMMON.

CLOTHING
LOCKERS WEAR THE MOST EXTRAVAGANT OUTFITS OF THE STREET DANCES
MENTIONED IN THIS BOOK. BLACK AND WHITE HOOP-STRIPED T-SHIRTS AND
SOCKS ARE TRADITIONAL. HOOP-STRIPED SOCKS, PANTALOONS TO THE KNEE,
BRITCHES – OFTEN WITH BRACES – ARE ALL STILL COMMONPLACE.

HEADWEAR
NEWSBOY/BARROWBOY HATS OR LARGE-BRIM HAVANAS ARE THE USUAL STYLE FOR LOCKERS.

HIP HOP

WHAT IS IT?

Get ready to vibe and socialize with this hype dance style. Whether you're at home or in a club, these moves will get you started and ready to show and prove. We've got some tracks for you to practise to on page 108, and expert advice from Clara throughout the section.

THE MOVES

WATCH THE › ‹ **VIDEO HERE**

2-STEP

THE 2-STEP COMES UP IN A LOT OF DANCE STYLES, AND THERE ARE A FEW VARIATIONS IN HIP HOP DANCE, BUT HERE'S THE BASIC ONE TO GET YOU STARTED.

01

Start with your feet together and arms resting by your sides.

02

Raise your left leg from the knee, using your arms for balance.

03

Step your left foot out to the left and place it on the ground as your right arm straightens out to the right and your left arm crosses your body.

04

Raise your left leg again at the knee, bringing your foot back to the centre, using your arms for balance.

05

Return your feet together and rest your arms by your sides.

CABBAGE PATCH

YOU'LL PROBABLY RECOGNIZE THIS MOVE AS IT'S A REALLY POPULAR ONE. THE GUCCI CREW II RELEASED A SONG DESCRIBING IT.

01

Start with your feet together and arms resting by your sides.

02

Turn your body to the right-hand side while stretching your arms out to the right and turning your right hip out to the side. Raise your right leg at the knee.

03

Shift from your left foot on to your right, pulling your arms in towards you at the same time. Your body should still be pointing to the right.

04

Change feet again, this time shifting on to your left foot, and push your arms out straight in front of you so you are back in the same position as step 2.

05

Swinging your arms in a semi-circle to the left, step on to your right foot, turning your body to face fowards as you do so.

06

As you keep turning, change feet again, this time shifting on to your left foot. Keep your arms out straight in front of you.

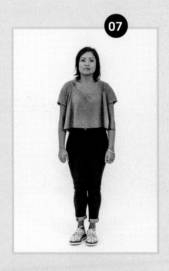

07

Turn right so you are facing forwards, as in step 1. Place your feet together and lower your arms to rest by your sides.

To repeat the move follow the steps again, substituting 'left' where it says 'right' and 'right' where it says 'left'.

WATCH THE › ‹ VIDEO HERE

KICK BALL CHANGE

THIS IS ANOTHER MOVE THAT CROPS UP IN A LOT OF DANCE STYLES. FOR THIS HIP HOP VERSION, CLARA SAYS, 'KEEP IT NICE AND LOOSE SO IT HAS A BOUNCY FEEL TO IT.'

01

02

03

Start with your feet together and arms resting by your sides. To show this move clearly, Clara is pictured side-on, but you don't have to turn to the side.

Lift your left leg up at the knee and bring your right arm up, bending at the elbow.

Kick your left foot out in front of you.

04

Bring your left leg back in at the knee.

05

Return your left foot to the floor.

06

Step your right foot behind you, leaning back from the waist. Extend your right arm straight down and bring your left arm up at the elbow.

07

Step your right foot back to the centre and stand up straight, resting your arms by your sides.

To repeat the move follow the steps again, substituting 'left' where it says 'right' and 'right' where it says 'left'.

WATCH THE › ‹ VIDEO HERE

ROBOCOP

SEEN THE MOVIE? IF SO, YOU'LL KNOW WHO THIS WAS NAMED AFTER. MOST WORK HERE IS IN THE UPPER BODY, BUT KEEP THE REST OF THE MOVEMENT CLEAN FOR THE BEST EFFECT.

01 Start with your feet together and arms resting by your sides.

02 This is a preparation step for step 3. Bring your left arm into your chest, at the same time slightly raising your left heel.

03

Step your right foot out to the side as you lower your left elbow down and in to your side, while simultaneously raising your right elbow up and out to the right-hand side.

04

Step your feet together and, keeping your arms bent at the elbow, bring them into a straight line across your chest.

05

Raise your right elbow up and out to the right-hand side as you lower your left elbow down and in to your side.

06

Step your left foot out to the side as you lower your right elbow down and in to your side, while simultaneously raising your left elbow up and out to the left-hand side.

07

Step your feet together and, keeping your arms bent at the elbow, bring them into a straight line across your chest.

08

Lower your arms to rest at your sides.

WATCH THE › ‹ VIDEO HERE

ROGER RABBIT

TO KEEP THIS MOVE FLUID, MAKE SURE THAT YOUR ARMS ARE NICE AND LOOSE.

01

Start with your feet together and arms resting by your sides.

02

Push your arms out behind you. At the same time, hop on to your left foot and swing your right leg out behind you.

03

Bring your arms forwards and step your right foot behind and to the left of your left foot in a cross.

04

Hop on to your right foot and swing your left foot out in front of you. At the same time, bring your arms out in front of you.

05

Swing your left leg behind you and again bring your arms behind you.

06

Bring your arms forwards and step your left foot behind and to the right of your right foot in a cross.

07

Hop on to your left foot and kick your right foot forwards. At the same time, bring your arms out in front of you.

08

Step your feet together and let your arms rest by your sides.

WATCH THE › ‹ VIDEO HERE

KRISS KROSS

CLARA SAYS, 'THIS IS A FUN MOVE. KEEP THE BOUNCE IN THE STEP AND REMEMBER TO PULL YOUR ARMS BACK ON THE CROSS.'

01

Stand straight with your feet hip-width apart and arms resting by your sides.

02

Jump your feet apart on your toes and lift your arms 45 degrees away from your body.

03

Cross your left leg behind your right, turning your right foot so the toe is pointing outwards. At the same time, lift your arms at the elbows until they reach an angle of roughly 90 degrees to your body.

04

Jump your feet apart on your toes and lift your arms 45 degrees away from your body.

05

Cross your right leg behind your left leg, turning your left foot so the toe is pointing outwards. At the same time, lift your arms at the elbows until they reach an angle of roughly 90 degrees to your body.

06

Uncross your feet, stand straight, and drop your hands to your sides.

WATCH THE › ‹ VIDEO HERE

RUNNING MAN

IMAGINE YOURSELF RUNNING ON THE SPOT WITH THIS MOVE. LATER ON YOU CAN MOVE AROUND A LITTLE, BUT WHILE YOU'RE LEARNING IT'S BEST TO STAY ON ONE SPOT.

01

Start with your feet together and arms resting by your sides. To show this move clearly, Clara is pictured side-on, but you don't have to turn to the side for the move.

02

Lift your arms at the elbows and raise your right knee.

03

Lower your right foot to the ground in front of you and lift your left heel off the ground, raising your elbows so they are at right angles to your body.

04

Straighten up onto your right leg and bring your left leg forwards so it is bent at the knee in front of you. At the same time, lower your arms slightly, keeping your elbows bent.

05

Step your left foot forwards and raise your forearms until they are parallel to the floor.

06

Straighten up onto your left leg and bring your right leg forwards so it is bent at the knee in front of you. At the same time, lower your arms slightly, keeping your elbows bent.

07

Lower your right foot to the ground in front of you and lift your left heel off the ground, raising your elbows so they are at right angles to your body.

08

Straighten up onto your right leg and bring your left leg forwards so it is bent at the knee in front of you. At the same time, lower your arms slightly, keeping your elbows bent.

09

Lower your left foot to the ground next to your right foot, and your arms to your sides.

WATCH THE › ‹ VIDEO HERE

RUNNING MAN ARMS OUT

REPEAT THE RUNNING MAN (ON PAGES 96–97) BUT ON STEPS 2, 4, 6, AND 8 REACH YOUR ARMS IN FRONT OF YOU AND ON 3, 5, AND 7 PULL YOUR ELBOWS BACK TO SHOULDER LEVEL.

01

02

03

STEVE MARTIN

THE STEVE MARTIN WAS DEVELOPED AFTER A MOVE THE ACTOR OF THE SAME NAME PULLED IN ONE OF HIS MOVIES. THERE'S EVEN A SONG CALLED 'THE STEVE MARTIN' BY EPMD.

01

Start with your feet together and arms resting by your sides.

02

Jump to face left, landing on your left foot, with your right leg bending at the knee behind you. Lift your arms at the elbows so they are at right angles to your body.

03

Jump back to the centre, again landing on your left foot, rotating your right knee out to the side. At the same time, straighten out your arms.

04

Jump to the right, your weight still on your left foot. Lift your right leg up at the knee in front of you. At the same time lift your arms at the elbows so they are at right angles to your body.

05

Lower your right foot to the floor and your arms to your sides.

06

Jump on to your right foot and lift your left foot behind you, bending your left leg at the knee.

07

Jump back to the centre, again landing on your right foot and turn your left knee out to the side. At the same time, lower your arms.

08

Jump to the left, keeping your weight on your right foot, and bend your left knee up. At the same time, lift your elbows up at right angles to your body.

09

Jump back to the centre, landing with your feet together and your arms by your sides.

WATCH THE › ‹ VIDEO HERE

JANET

THIS IS NAMED AFTER THE ONE AND ONLY JANET JACKSON. SHE USED A LOT OF HIP HOP MOVES IN HER MUSIC VIDEOS. CHECK 'EM OUT!

01

Stand straight with your arms resting by your sides.

02

Swing your arms to the right and lift your left leg out to the side.

03

Place the toe of your left foot on the floor, keeping the heel raised. As your arms reach an angle of 90 degrees, bend your wrists so your fingers are pointing up.

04

Lower the heel of your left foot to the floor, bringing your weight forwards. At the same time, your right heel should come off the floor and your right knee will slightly bend. Straighten your wrists.

05

Step your right toe in next to your left foot and – keeping your arms straight – bend your wrists so your fingers are pointing down to the floor.

06

Shift your weight on to your right leg and bend your left knee. At the same time, straighten your wrists.

07

Lower your left toe to the floor and bend your wrists so your fingers are pointing up.

08

Step your weight on to your left leg, raise your right heel and straighten your wrists.

09

Step your right toe in to your left foot and - keeping your arms straight - bend your wrists so your fingers are pointing down to the floor.

10

Turn your feet and body back to the centre, with your feet together, and rest your arms by your sides.

To do the Reverse Janet, use the same steps as the Janet, but exchange 'right' for 'left' and 'left' for 'right'.

BART SIMPSON

LIKE A LOT OF HIP HOP MOVES, THIS ONE IS NAMED AFTER THE CHARACTER WHO INSPIRED IT – IN THIS CASE, IT MIMICS BART'S FUNNY WAY OF MOVING.

01

Start with your feet together and arms resting by your sides.

02

Bending your arms at the elbows, raise them until they are at right angles to your body. In preparation for the next move, keep your elbows where they are and lower your forearms to chest height.

03

Step your left foot out to the left, pressing your toe into the ground and raising your heel. At the same time, extend your right arm out to the side and bring your left arm across your chest, still bent at the elbow.

04

Step your left foot back to the centre and return your arms to the centre, keeping them bent at the elbows.

05

Raise your forearms so they are at 90-degree angles to your upper arms.

06

Keeping your elbows where they are, lower your forearms to chest height.

07

Step your right foot to the right. At the same time, extend your left arm to the side and bring your right arm across your chest.

08

Step your right foot back to the centre and return your arms to the centre, keeping them bent at the elbow.

09

Raise your forearms so they are at 90 degrees to your upper arms.

10

Lower your arms right down, and let your hands rest by your sides.

DJ HOOCH'S TOP 10 TRACKS

BIG DADDY KANE – 'AIN'T NO HALF STEPPIN''

BRAND NUBIAN – 'ALL FOR ONE'

CHUBB ROCK – 'TREAT 'EM RIGHT'

HEAVY D & THE BOYZ –' YOU CAN'T SEE WHAT I CAN SEE'

LORDS OF THE UNDERGROUND – 'CHIEF ROCKA'

MAIN SOURCE – 'FAKIN' THE FUNK'

NAUGHTY BY NATURE – 'UPTOWN ANTHEM'

NICE & SMOOTH – 'HIP HOP JUNKIES'

BLACK MOON – 'WHO GOT THE PROPS'

LEADERS OF THE NEW SCHOOL – 'CASE OF THE P.T.A'

WHAT'S GOOD TO WEAR?

FOOTWEAR
TIMBERLANDS OR DR. MARTENS WERE THE FOOTWEAR OF CHOICE FOR MOST HIP HOP DANCERS
FROM THE 1990'S. SNEAKERS ARE THE FOOTWEAR OF CHOICE FOR TODAY'S HIP HOP DANCER.

CLOTHING
FOR ORIGINAL HIP HOP STYLE, THINK TLC (IF YOU'RE FEMALE) OR
NAUGHTY BY NATURE (IF YOU'RE A GUY): LOOSE JEANS; BIG, THROWBACK
AMERICAN-BASKETBALL OR FOOTBALL JERSEYS; DUNGAREES.

HEADWEAR
BACK IN THE DAY YOU'D ACCESSORIZE WITH A FLAT-TOP HAIR-DO,
BUT NOW ROCK A CAP AS YOUR CROWN!

HOUSE

WHAT IS IT?

House style came out of the club scene in Chicago and New York in the 1980s, and later got picked up in a major way by clubs in Paris. It wasn't until more recently that it emerged from the underground scene and was adopted by mainstream groups. The queen of house, Clara Bajado, will show you the foundation steps in this chapter, to get you into this soulful dance style.

THE MOVES

WATCH THE › ‹ VIDEO HERE

CROSSROADS

CLARA SAYS, 'KEEP THE CROSS IN THIS MOVE NICE AND CLEAR WHEN YOU'RE LEARNING IT SO YOU DON'T GET YOURSELF IN A TANGLE.'

01

Stand with your hands resting by your sides and feet hip-width apart.

02

Cross your right foot behind your left foot. Keep your arms loose and let your torso follow in with your steps.

03

Step your left foot back, out of the cross.

Cross your right foot in front of your left foot. Keep your arms loose and let your torso follow in with your steps.

Step your left foot forwards, out of the cross.

Cross your right foot behind your left foot. Keep your arms loose and let your torso follow in with your steps.

Bring your left foot next to your right foot, stand straight and return your arms to your sides.

WATCH THE › ‹ **VIDEO HERE**

FARMER

THE FARMER MOVE HAS DIFFERENT ORIGINS, APPEARING IN FOLK DANCES AND AFRICAN AND CARIBBEAN DANCES. LATINOS USED TO CALL IT THE 'CABALLERO'.

01

Stand with your hands resting by your sides and feet hip-width apart.

02

Bend your knees, keeping them loose as you get ready to spring into a hop on to your left foot.

03

Begin the hop by bringing your right knee up, using your arms naturally to keep your balance.

04

The momentum of your hop should spring you up into the air, your right knee raised but your left leg still straight, with toes pointing down to the ground.

05

Bend your knees as you land, with your weight spread evenly between your feet so you are ready to hop again.

06

Begin the hop by bringing your left knee up, using your arms naturally to keep your balance.

07

The momentum of your hop should spring you up into the air, your left knee raised but your right leg still straight, with toes pointing down to the ground.

08

Bend your knees as you land, using your arms to balance yourself.

09

Stand straight, returning your arms to your sides.

WATCH THE › ‹ VIDEO HERE

HEEL-TOE

THE HEEL-TOE IS A MOVE THAT LOOKS GOOD IF YOU CAN MASTER IT AND MAKE IT LOOK SMOOTH.

01

Stand with your hands resting by your sides and feet hip-width apart.

02

Put your right leg straight out in front of you, touching the heel of your right foot to the ground. Keep your arms loose and let your torso lean forwards.

Now lift your right foot and, bending your right leg at the knee, tap your toe to the ground next to your left heel.

Placing your right foot to the ground, stretch your left leg straight out in front of you, touching the heel of your left foot to the ground. Keep your arms loose and let your torso lean forwards.

Now lift your left foot and, bending your left leg at the knee, tap your toe to the ground next to your right heel. Allow your torso to lean slightly backwards.

Lower your left heel to the ground, bringing your feet together and return your arms to your sides.

WATCH THE › ‹ VIDEO HERE

JACK IN THE BOX

THIS MOVE IS ONE OF THE BASIC MOVES OF HOUSE DANCE. KEEP THE MOVE SMOOTH, NOT JERKING YOUR CHEST AS YOU MOVE FORWARDS AND BACKWARDS.

01

Stand with your hands resting by your sides and feet hip-width apart.

02

Bend your knees and sink your weight through your sitting bones, with your toes pointing out.

03

Straighten your legs gradually and lean your torso backwards, with a curve in your back coming through from your hips.

04

Straighten your back and in one movement lean forwards, keeping your back rounded. Keep your arms nice and loose.

05

Straighten your back and let your arms rest by your sides.

WATCH THE › 〈 VIDEO HERE

PAS DE BOURRÉE

THIS MOVE COMES FROM THE WORLD OF BALLET. A QUICK TIP FROM CLARA: 'MAKE SURE YOU DO A PROPER CROSS WHEN THE STEP TELLS YOU TO, AND KEEP ON YOUR TOES.'

01

Stand with your hands resting by your sides and feet hip-width apart.

02

Cross your right foot behind your left foot, using your arms for balance.

03

Step your left foot back to the left.

04

Turning your torso slightly to the right, step your right foot to the side, knee bent.

05

Making sure your weight is on your right leg, cross your left foot behind your right foot, using your arms to balance.

06

Step your right foot to the right.

07

Turning your torso slightly to the left, step your left foot to the side, knee bent.

08

Pivot slightly on the ball of your left foot so you are facing forwards and bring your right foot in to your left, resting your arms by your sides.

SKATING

NO SURPRISES AS TO HOW THIS MOVE GOT ITS NAME. CLARA SAYS, 'KEEP IT NICE AND SMOOTH SO YOU LOOK LIKE YOU ARE ACTUALLY SKATING.'

01 Stand with your hands resting by your sides and feet hip-width apart.

02 Bending at your elbow, raise your right forearm in front of you so it's at a 45-degree angle and raise your right heel slightly in anticipation of the next step.

03

Straighten your right arm out to the right so it's at a 45-degree angle to your body. At the same time step your right foot out to the side, parallel to your arm. Bend your left knee slightly and bring your left arm back for balance.

04

Step your right foot back to the centre and return your arms to your sides. Bend your left elbow to raise your left forearm so it's at a 45-degree angle and raise your left heel slightly in anticipation of the next step.

05

Straighten your left arm out to the left so it's at a 45-degree angle to your body. At the same time, step your left foot out to the side, parallel to your arm. Bend your right knee slightly and bring your right arm back for balance.

06

Step your left foot back to the centre and return both arms to your sides.

WATCH THE › [QR CODE] ‹ VIDEO HERE

SHUFFLE

THIS MOVE APPEARS IN LOTS OF DANCE STYLES. HERE IT GETS A HOUSE TWIST. CLARA SAYS, 'KEEP YOUR HEEL-TOE MOVES CLEAN AND QUICK SO THE MOVE LOOKS SHARP.'

01 Stand straight with your arms resting by your sides.

02 Hop on to your left foot, kicking your right leg out in front and slightly to the right, using your arms for balance. Your torso should face your kicking leg.

03

Now hop on to your right foot, kicking your left leg out in front and slightly to the left, using your arms for balance. Your torso should face your kicking leg.

04

Step your left foot behind your right foot in a cross, and turn your right foot out so your toes point right. Turn your torso slightly to the right as you do so.

05

Now facing to the right, slide your left foot behind you in a semi-circle, using your arms for balance.

06

Hop on to your right foot, bringing yourself to face front, and kick your left leg out in front of you and to the left, using your arms for balance.

07

Hop on to your left foot, kicking your right leg forwards and to the right. Use your arms for balance.

08

Step your right foot behind your left foot in a cross, turning your left foot out so your toes point left. Turn your torso slightly to the left as you do so.

09

Now facing to the left, slide your right foot behind you in a semi-circle, using your arms for balance.

10

Step your feet together.

TRAIN

CLARA HAS BEEN PICTURED SIDEWAYS ON FOR THIS MOVE SO YOU CAN SEE THE STEPS CLEARLY.

01

Stand with your hands resting by your sides and feet hip-width apart.

02

With a slight shift of both feet, bring your right foot forwards and raise your left arm slightly as your right arm moves behind you.

Raise your right heel off the ground and bend your knee slightly as you do so. Raise your left arm slightly at the same time.

Lift your right foot off the ground, bending your left knee and raising your left arm, still keeping it bent at the elbow. You are almost in a sitting position.

Lower your right toe to the ground and straighten your back to prepare for step 6.

With a slight shift of both feet, bring your left foot forwards and raise your right arm slightly as your left arm moves behind you.

07

Raise your left heel off the ground and bend your knee slightly as you do so. Raise your right arm slightly at the same time.

08

Lift your left foot off the ground, bending your right knee and raising your right arm, still keeping it bent at the elbow. You are almost in a sitting position.

09

Lower your left toe to the ground and straighten your back.

10

Bring your left foot in line with your right and let your arms fall loose at your sides.

DJ HOOCH'S TOP 10 TRACKS

ONUR OZMAN – 'IN THE CITY'

6TH BOROUGH PROJECT – 'B.U.R.T. (INSIDE)'

YONURICAN – 'BORIKEN SOUL'

OSUN LADE – 'MOMMA'S GROOVE'

MAYA JANE COLES – 'WHAT THEY SAY'

CRYSTAL WATERS – 'GYPSY WOMAN'

DENNIS FERRER – 'HEY HEY'

FISH GO DEEP – 'CURE AND THE CURSE'

JAMIROQUAI – 'SPACE COWBOY' REMIX

TOM NOVY – 'I DIDN'T WANT NOBODY'

WHAT'S GOOD TO WEAR?

FOOTWEAR
ANY FORM OF FOOTWEAR.

CLOTHING
HOUSE DANCERS TRADITIONALLY WORE VERY BAGGY CLOTHES –
LOOSE-FITTING JEANS AND LONG-SLEEVED, LOOSE T-SHIRTS.
NOW YOU SHOULD WEAR WHATEVER YOU FEEL COMFORTABLE IN.

HEADWEAR
HOUSE ISN'T A PARTICULARLY STYLIZED FORM OF DANCE; THE EMPHASIS
IS ON CLOTHES THAT ALLOW EASE OF MOVEMENT AND FLOW.

DIRECTORY

STOCKISTS

Universal Streetworks
http://www.universalstreetworks.com

Chief Rocka Clothing
https://www.chief-rocka.com/

The Legits
http://www.thelegits.com/

Biggest and Baddest
Stocked by The Bboy Spot
http://www.bboyspot.com

Serious
http://serious-brand.org

Mounfunk
http://www.mounfunk.com/
Mounfunk
c/o Six Step GmbH
Asternstr. 49 A
30167 Hannover

Armory
http://www.armoryhiphop.com/
Armory Survival Gear
803 F St.
San Diego, Ca. 92101

GLOBAL EVENTS

UK BBoy Championships
http://bboychampionships.com/

R16 World B-Boy Masters Championship
http://www.r16korea.com
Korea

Chelles Battle Pro
http://www.battle-pro.com/
France

Juste Deboute
http://www.juste-debout.com/fr_FR
France

The Notorious IBE
http://www.thenotoriousibe.com/
The Netherlands

Battle of the Year
http://www.battleoftheyear.de/
Germany

Outbreak
http://www.thebboyspot.com/outbreak/
Slovakia

Red Bull BC One
http://www.redbullbcone.com/

Freestyle Session
http://www.freestylesession.com/
USA

INDEX

PICTURE CREDITS

Pages 2, 6, 9, 13, 41, 42, 63, 64, 81, 82, 109,
132-3, 142, 143 NAKI © DJ Hooch.
Page 10 NATHAN STEPHEN aka MELO NS © DJ Hooch.
Page 11 MAURICE VAN DER MEIJS © DJ Hooch.
Page 14 KIEN QUAN © DJ Hooch.
Page 110 © Benjoy for BlackJack.
Page 131 © Innocent Adriko.
Page 141 Nika Kramer © IBE.
All step-by-steps © Haraala Hamilton.

ACKNOWLEDGMENTS

THANKS TO EVERYBODY WHO HELPED
MAKE THIS BOOK HAPPEN:

Brooke Milliner, Roxy Milliner, Sunni Brummitt,
Clara Bajado, Hannah Knowles and all at Octopus,
Julia Bell, Max, and Rob Pountney.

To the pioneers that laid the foundations of
the dance styles, we pay respect.

To the dancers worldwide pushing the boundaries
of what the human body can do, we salute you!

Keep on dancing like no one is watching!

PROMOTER, DJ, MUSIC LOVER, AND STREET-CULTURE JUNKIE, HOOCH HAS PLAYED AND PROMOTED CLUBS AND PARTIES ALL OVER LONDON FROM UNDERGROUND WAREHOUSE PARTIES TO SOME OF THE BIGGEST EVENTS AT THE CITY'S MAJOR VENUES. HE WAS PART OF THE INFAMOUS FUNKIN' PUSSY CREW WHO ROCKED PARTIES AND CLUBS IN LONDON AND ACROSS THE UK FOR OVER 20 YEARS!

ABOUT THE AUTHOR

Hooch had the longest-running weekly funk and hip hop club in the UK from 1991 to 2003 in Covent Garden's Africa Centre, London. He also brought over funk legends Parliament Funkadelic for some incredible gigs in the early 90's. The stars passed through undercover, the crowds kept coming and everyone kept dancing! Around the same time, the bboys (breakdancers) started hitting the club to get the beats they weren't getting elsewhere.

In 1996, Hooch started the Bboy Championships, which has run every year since. He also works as a consultant with major blue chip firms and TV production companies, organises world class bboy/hip hop projects and events, founded the first dedicated street dance studio (Breakstation), runs an events company (Hooch Events), and owns the online hip hop store and clothing label Universal Street Works. If that sounds busy, Hooch still DJs most weekends as well!

An Hachette UK Company
www.hachette.co.uk

First published in Great Britain in 2015 by
Cassell, a division of
Octopus Publishing Group Ltd
Carmelite House
50 Victoria Embankment
London EC4Y 0DZ
www.octopusbooks.co.uk
www.octopusbooksusa.com

Distributed in the US by
Hachette Book Group
1290 Avenue of the Americas
4th and 5th Floors
New York, NY 10020

Distributed in Canada by
Canadian Manda Group
664 Annette St.
Toronto, Ontario, Canada M6S 2C8

ISBN 978 1 84403 840 4

A CIP catalogue record for this book is available
from the British Library.

Printed and bound in China

10 9 8 7 6 5 4 3 2 1

Commissioning Editor - Hannah Knowles
Editor - Pollyanna Poulter
Copy Editor - Emma Hill
Proofreader - Jane Birch
Indexer - Isobel McLean
Design Manager - Jaz Bahra
Layout Design - Paul Sethi
In-house Design - Isabel de Cordova
Photography - Haarala Hamilton
Production Controller - Sarah-Jayne Johnson